Being WITH God...

RUTH HAMMOND

First published in 2017

Free Reign Books
freereignbooks@gmail.com
929 Waingaro Rd,
RD1, Ngaruawahia,
New Zealand.

© Free Reign Books
© Ruth Hammond

www.softwhispersbook.co.nz

ISBN 978-0-473-46231-4 PBK
ISBN 978-0-473-40003-3 HCR
ISBN 978-0-473-46181-2 EPUB

Graphic Design—The Zoo.
Editing by Sue Beguely—Triplecoil Script.
Ingram Spark 2018 listing uploaded by
Wild Side Publishing, wildsidepublishing.com

All rights reserved.

This book may not be copied, reproduced or transferred by any means whatsoever without the written consent of Ruth Hammond.

Please direct any queries to Ruth Hammond:
hello@softwhispersbook.com

THIS IS A BEAUTIFUL PERSONAL REFLECTION of Ruth's journey into a deeper understanding and experience of God. With gentle simplicity, as she shares the thoughts of her heart, her wisdom 'rings bells' of understanding, and prompts us into graceful reflection on our own relationship with the God who is Love.

-THE VERY REV'D PETER BECK. RETIRED DEAN OF TARANAKI/PIRIHI MATAMUA O TARANAKI

The essence of this new book ... is an "Intimacy between Ruth and her Lord". Her words inspire and quicken the Holy Spirit within, recalling moments of intimacy with Him. This is a book compelling the reader to be totally involved until 'put down'. **IT IS A BOOK OF BLESSING TO EXPERIENCE.**

-THE REV. ELIZ RICHARDS, RETIRED PRISON CHAPLAIN

Ruth Hammond is a listener, listening to God, and from this **CONVEYS PROFOUND SPIRITUAL TRUTHS OF THE FAITH.** She writes with prayerful and pastoral sensitivity 'from the heart' of her own experiences, yet the reader will surely identify with her experiences of life.

-THE REV DEREK LIGHTBOURNE. PASTOR, MENTOR AND FRIEND

Ruth Hammond has developed another God-inspired book to bring **INSPIRATION AND HOPE.** These intimate insights and poetic writings share a remarkable depth as she reflects on her own spiritual experiences. 'Being with God ...' will encourage and uplift readers in their own God conversations, and ultimately act as a spiritual signpost that points us all to Jesus.

- JUSTIN ST. VINCENT. PRESIDENT OF NZ CHRISTIAN WRITERS

ONCE AGAIN GOD SPEAKS to the author of this book, as she responds faithfully and eagerly to the 'nudges' God gives, when He wants her to write more of her life experiences. She understands that she has a specific role to play, just as we all have in this life. It is in the seeking and discovering of this role that she fulfils the destiny He had always and forever laid out for her. **THERE IS SO MUCH TO EXPLORE IN SEARCHING THIS BOOK.** Phrases such as "silence that talks" and "reality is now is forever" and finally the thought that "people have only discovered a small amount of God's creation ... there is so much more", are encouraging and exciting. She finally shares her understanding that, "the baseline of our existence is 'at-one-ment' with God and our time here is to discover this."

-CAROL LINFOOT FOY

I asked ...

God, many people find it hard to find you. Does it have to be so difficult to find you?

He answered ...

Just think of me and there I am. I am within your mind and your heart, listening and waiting for you to tune into my still, quiet voice.

Contents

This all began ... 8
Draw close to me ... 12
Growth in understanding ... 18
Walking the beach together ... 21
Time, seasons and paradox ... 23
Awe and reverence ... 25
Insights can be invisible ... 26
Wanting to know more ... 27
Drawn to the garden ... 30
Softly, softly as falling rain ... 31
Atonement and being in at-one-ment ... 32
At-one-ment is the essence of being ... 36
At-one-ment for the world ... 38
Follow your own calling ... 40
From the edge of the beach ... 43
At-one-ment in simplicity ... 44
Stronger for having been weak ... 46
Gifts singular and merging ... 49
All is contained in whoever ... 52
An Easter Sunday conversation ... 54
I lay down my life of my own accord ... 56
Wealth that disturbs me: a paradox emerges ... 58
Marvelling but not necessarily recognising ... 61
Grief and loss can bring birth ... 65
Powerlessness can birth strength ... 67
Where is it, this closeness to God? ... 70
Silent yet loud attention-getters ... 71
The falcon stood ... 73
Many people find it difficult to find you ... 75
Love dissolves fear ... 78
Prayer is not duty-bound ... 80
The dance of the known and the unknown ... 82
An eternal love ... 83
Still and deep from me to you ... 86

This all began

...

early one morning as I was thinking about the nudge I thought God had given me. I often chat with God. It usually starts with me talking to him. Occasionally God has something to say that comes into my mind like a thought. I just know within my heart that I am to take notice and write it down.

Recently, God seemed to be telling me he wanted me to write another book. Another book! Now that was an idea I hadn't thought about. Out came the pen and paper. This was serious. I knew I needed to record our conversations.

THE INITIAL CONVERSATION WENT LIKE THIS:

> Lord, I feel that you want me to write again ... yet another book. Am I hearing correctly?
>
> **Yes, you are. Others are waiting for more encouragement through you. Trust me. Trust my spirit. As in the desert, I am in the air to be breathed.**
>
> **Already you have discovered I am in the desert places of your life. I want you to write about your challenges and the spiritual experiences you have had. You know I am in the 'letting go', the quiet places and the 'unknowing'. When you stepped into those places and trusted me, you found me.**

So I waited ...

      until one day ...

Lord, I notice that your nudges often carry me to places I would never have dreamt of going ... or they take thought and courage to obey. Is this part of the pattern of listening to you which I am to follow and share in obedience?

Yes, it is. I call you to traverse water, as it were, while I provide the stepping stones. I know you think such water is deep and with a very swift current. However, I provide stable stepping stones at the right depth so you can walk across them without losing your balance.

Now I'm mentally seeing a picture of deep, dark, rushing water that I step out into without seeing the stones until I've started to take the first step. The stones are strong ... solid ... so strong and so solid ... while the water is rushing towards a calm, tranquil lake. This lake is extremely beautiful. It is large and not deep at all. My overview is interesting. I am coming down from the mountain places and want to cross a narrow gorge of deep, rushing water to get to the other side where there is a safe shore. I'm really intrigued because I can't swim. Is that why I get that picture? Why my obedience to you is to let go in total dependency and trust? Am I to step into the place of drowning to self and my own competency ... to step into the place of nothingness in order to be with you?

Yes, that is why you have that picture. You and I both know you can't swim. However, I don't ask you to swim. I supply you with stones that you can walk upon. It's all about trusting me as you listen to me.

Is that what happened the day I found my son Greg dead from his heart attack? Unknowingly I stepped into the deepest darkest cavern of my life and there you were. Within the same second of discovering him dead you provided me with stepping stones of peace and strength. Have I understood correctly that you were there when that was happening?

Yes, you are seeing the links. My purpose for you is to do more writing in order that others may be encouraged to listen to me and to trust me. You have discovered how to observe the little things as well as the big things in your ordinary, everyday life. You see that I am able to be discerned. I am there. Keep on looking for me. It is often in hindsight that you see me best. I am calling you to share something new with your book. It is to speak of knowing pain and how my love can be a balm in the midst of such pain. Your pains are scattered on a path along which I have travelled with you. You also know joy. Keep writing. All the threads will tie together.

Draw close to me ...

Draw close to me
I understand your pain
which you can't catch or even touch.

Its depths are too deep to find.
I am in that pain,
I know it.

By drawing close to me
your pain will ease
as we share it in my spirit.

Once again I knew that God knew ...

Two months later ...

my curiosity about writing got the better of me ...
I asked,

> Where shall I begin with this book? I get the feeling you want me to tell others about how I listen to you – the chatting and the quiet times. Is that right?

Quietly, an answer came into my mind ...

> **Yes, it is. I do want you to write another book. I will tell you when to start writing.**

So I waited again ...
Then one morning when I was in the shower, the first words came ...

> **There are ... so many ways ... of being with God.**

I dressed, mulling those words over in my mind. Yes! The moment had come to put pen to paper. It was amusing to think I had thought the first words would come on a day I could set aside in peace and quiet, to listen to – and chat with – God.

Really amusing!

For there I was in the middle of a Christmas-New Year gathering with fourteen other members of our extended family!

Quiet? Peaceful? Still? A retreat from others?

No way!

I settled to write while the activity cascaded around me.

I muttered quietly under my breath,

> Lord, I heard the start – but where do I begin?

It was as if my mind was empty. Then suddenly ...

> **At the beginning. Start at the beginning.**

> I can't remember my beginning. I can't even remember my first thoughts of my awareness of my existence.

> **Start where you remember your first thoughts about me. How did you hear about me? Share the steps that emerged in your life.**

> Lord, you know it all. For me, I think it must have arisen out of a promise my parents made to each other when they married.

Marriage between people from different streams of Christianity were often experienced as being divisive 70 to 80 years ago. Divisions between denominations were quite marked. My mother was a Roman Catholic. My father was a Presbyterian. They compromised by marrying in the Anglican Church. To this day I don't know any living relatives of my mother, or even their names.

After they married, only my mother's father and her brother kept in touch. The rest of her Roman Catholic family considered she had committed the ultimate sin. In their minds our family was doomed to eternal rejection by God and so they rejected us as well. I thought writing down this aside was important as an explanation for the reader. I wasn't expecting the question that followed.

You know that I never abandoned or rejected you, don't you?

Yes. Of that I am certain. You have shown me in so many ways that your love is indestructible. You have shown me you are constantly with us. We only have to think of you, and there you are ... ready to listen.

So start where you first remember hearing about me.

I think it was when I was six or seven years of age. We lived in the country, far from a village or a church. My parents decided I needed to hear about you, so they organised religious correspondence lessons for me. Every week, Sunday school lessons came through the postal service. Bible stories came alive for me. I must have been just able to read, for I recall sitting alone reading the stories, answering questions and colouring in pictures. For me, answering the questions became tedious, but Mum and Dad insisted I continue.

Are you glad now that you did those lessons?

Oh, yes. Thank goodness they kept me at it. My lessons went to a teacher who replied each week and sent me the next lesson. I'm now grateful to her and to them. I've never thought about being thankful for those lessons before. My childhood memory of the weekly discipline is what is imprinted on my mind. Now I'm sorry I never expressed my thanks to you, or to them, for the opportunity I was given.

So now you see it. I knew you would one day. It just took time and reflection, like everything else that happens in a person's life. I am there in everything, if you look for me. You can even see hidden wisdom ... if you look for it. However, I know you have another childhood memory that has stayed with you for life because of those lessons. It was when you read about the time I was in a boat with my disciples during a storm. That story spoke to you. Tell me how it affected you and what you did about it.

You're right. That story did speak to me about believing in you. Now I think you expected the disciples to have enough faith in God to believe that everything would be all right. As a child I thought your expectation was for the disciples to speak to the wind and the waves with the same authority you did, and that the storm would become still for them as it did for you. In my heart, I believed in you so strongly, I thought I would put it to the test. The day came when a storm was battering the trees around the garden where I often danced for you. It was like a glade, surrounded by trees and I loved going there. I would open my arms and dance, talking to you as I danced.

I remember. There was a joy and a freedom in your dance. You never knew how much that delighted me?

No, I've never thought about it from your point of view; a child dancing as she talked to you is so different from the earnestness of so many prayers you receive every day.

So tell what happened as a result of your trying to calm the wind.

Well, the wind didn't listen to me. It just kept blowing the leaves and the twigs off the trees.

And how did that affect you?

I thought it was a sign I didn't believe in you enough, or maybe you weren't always there listening to me, or your powers worked only for you, or that I wasn't good enough. I think it was the start of my experiences where I decided sometimes you answered prayer and sometimes you didn't.

Growth in understanding ...

LATER ON THAT EVENING ...

I'm aware your understanding of me has changed over time. Understanding of me is always open to change. Some call it growth, some call it development. What do you call it?

Wow, Lord! That's a question and a half. Yes, my understandings of you have changed over the span of my life. As I have journeyed with you I have learned more and more about you. At the same time I have learned more and more about myself. Somehow, the two are merged in a way that always has me learning at a pace I can cope with. I'd call it 'growth in insight'.

Let's take the boat in the storm story. Every now and then that childhood experience comes to mind. Flickers of childhood logic have lingered over the years ... and you've always dealt with them at my slow learning pace. For example, I've learned that you always listen to my prayers, listen with wisdom, but don't always answer them as I want you to. Answers emerge over time – often better answers – if I look at a whole overview and not just at my desire for an immediate quick fix. I seem to get new insights over time.

What else has emerged for you? I'm interested in what you were thinking this morning about the 'boat in the storm' story.

I'm interested too. For me, today, the story tells me to trust in you no matter what is going on around me. When I say 'you' I am talking about the whole of you: Father, Son and Holy Spirit. So much of my journey as we walk together is for me to hear, 'Trust me'. Lord, that's all I really need to hear. However, I seem to need to hear it in so many different situations. Thank you for your patience.

I suggest you go back and reread the story and then come back to me with what you see anew.

So I went back to Luke 8:22–25, Matthew 8:23–27 and Mark 4:36–41.

Lord, I went back to the different versions in my Bible. Today I am still focussing on trusting in you even when facing situations that feel like uninvited whirlwinds. That peaceful place where you are with me is similar to being in the eye of a hurricane. I know the fear of being in a boat during a storm. I would have been feeling the same as the disciples felt, if I had been there with them. I certainly would have been impressed with your command over the wind and the waves. From then on I would have felt safe travelling in a boat with you at any time. Strangely, it reminds me of a day in my life when that trust brought great peace.

You have had more than one of those moments in your life. Can you tell about the occasion you are thinking of?

I think I can. It was a bit of a surprise to me. It was about four years ago. I was travelling to hospital by ambulance. I remember thinking, This might be it. There's a possibility I might die.

Tell me about the bit that was a surprise.

Well, I was surprised at how calm and accepting of death I was. I felt OK about my relationship with you and that I would experience you in a new way. The real surprise was what emerged as being most important: in what state would I be leaving all my relationships on earth? I couldn't think of anyone with whom I had unfinished business or an unhappy relationship. There, right at the top of the list, the thing that seemed most important before leaving this life was how I had related to others. A huge sense of peace emerged in knowing I was at peace with others ... and because of that I could face meeting with you, knowing that peace.

So facing death could be like facing a tornado. Is that also what you're thinking?

In a way, yes. And in a way, no. It could be similar: there is always the unknown when experiencing a tornado. However, in the eye of the storm is the quiet place. You were in the peaceful place that came upon me unexpectedly. I recognised it then and I recognise it now.

I'm glad you saw me as a place of refuge. It's not the first time I've been thought of as a place of refuge.

The Old Testament scriptures talk about a place of refuge. However, my favourite picture of a place of refuge is where God said, 'See, I have carved a place for you in the palm of my hand.' Those words are so meaningful to me. The God who created the universe has carved a place in the palm of his hand for me. How great is that! It is almost more than my heart and mind can cope with. And nails carved places in your hands also when you died on the cross. How loving is that! I never cease to be amazed at the depth of your love. I don't have the words to express what I feel.

I think it's time for you to sleep now. You've done enough thinking for today!

I sipped the last sip of water, placed pen and paper on the bedside table along with my glasses and watch and finally turned out the light. The night encircled me as sleep overtook my wandering thoughts.

Walking the beach together ...

Hi, Lord. I think I just want to walk along the beach with you at the moment. I love the times when I imagine I'm paddling along the water's edge with you beside me. It's so good being close to you. I don't have to talk. You're just there. Little waves lap in and out. I'm aware I always place myself on the shallow side and have you on the deeper side. We can just be. When I stop to look out to sea I notice you stop too and patiently wait. There's such a sense of contentment being in your company, such a sense of belonging and being at ease. It really is a companionable silence that says everything that needs to be said.

I enjoy those times too. Silent communication is a loving way of being. Let's walk in the silence together for a few minutes. Put down your pen and be with me for a few minutes.

So down went the pen and we walked quietly along an imaginary beach. It was me who broke the silence.

It was so still, refreshing and peaceful when I stopped for those moments.

I know. It's good for me too. I also find it refreshing to take time out to be with you.

That's interesting. You are not limited by time. To me that means you can be with many folk at the same time. Somehow you can meet with us individually whilst at the same time you can experience us collectively. That's outside our capabilities.

Mmmm. True. The day will come when you can do it collectively. It has to do with how you are created. It also has to do with your understanding of time which restricts you now. Your senses only experience a small amount of my creation. There is so much more that you can't see, but that doesn't mean those things don't exist.

We talked about that on an earlier occasion. I think this is where I would like to share that conversation. Would that be OK with you?

Why not? It seems to fit and I don't see the point of me repeating myself.

I went back through my journal to find the conversation I was thinking of. To my surprise it had occurred three months previously. It seemed like only three weeks to me.

Time, seasons and paradox ...

I'm intrigued with the expression deep time. I've never known what to call it, so I call it eternal time: the time which covers all time before now, now, and all the time to come. To me, it is the overview of existence which you see but which we see only as our lifespan ... until we get a glimpse of your time.

Time is something humankind has measured relative to the movement of what you see: sun, moon, planets and stars ... things that seem to have stable patterns you can rely upon. Humans need time only in order to coordinate coming together: for example, meetings or travel. How you follow the seasons helps with planning for agriculture. Time is a tool humans have devised. The reality is that now is forever.

I'm OK with that. Life appears to have its seasons too. Yes, I'm in the second half of life—the second half of the second half of life, most likely. It seems as if the world values youth as being the most desirable time of life. It doesn't seem the best time to me. It seems to me as I have got older I prefer to be less: less status, less power, fewer things, fewer needs. Fewer wants seem so much more attractive. Is this yet another of the many milestones in life?

You are discovering much that makes sense to you. My logic is diametrically opposed to the usual logic of the world ... sort of upside down if you like. You still have much to learn, but you have discovered the peace that only comes from awareness of me. The world is discovering how the tiniest things hold the most power. There are even smaller things to be discovered that are tinier than most humans can imagine. I hold the paradox: I am the tiniest and I am the largest; I am in everything; I am in

you and you are in me; I am more than you can see beyond your knowing or your understanding. Just relax. The knowledge is just for me. What I love best is knowing you (humankind), and you (humankind) knowing me. Just being in at-one-ment ... free to be at one.

Thank you. I'm amazed you talk with me.

The conversation ended. As so frequently happens, I quietly eased into that mind-wandering place that precedes sleep.

Awe and reverence ...

Lord, what do you want me to learn next?

Just keep listening and obeying.

The walks on the water's edge, I love them. Do you want me to keep on taking those walks?

I love them also. Of course you can. Any moment you want to seek me there – just think me there – I will be with you. I understand you like companionable silence. I can be met in many ways.

Lord, it is very comfortable and one-to-one. It has a deep reverence but it isn't the worshipful adoration I believe you are worthy of. What are your thoughts about this?

The moments of deep awe and reverence are very powerful. The flashes of these have enormous power – a bit like the power contained in lightning strikes. They are enough for where you are at. Don't worry about the length of them. You have eternity for that.

Insights can be invisible ...

I was thinking it would be so easy to miss what you do in my life ... the things you show me and teach me. It seems normal to take things for granted. We often miss the significance of the signs that show you really care for us. Do you mean us to miss the evidence of you in our everyday lives?

No, I don't. But I do want to give you total free will so that if you want to discern me in action you can. I work in the little things in your everyday life – the things that you could take for granted. My ways are invisible if you don't want to see them. They are right in front of you if you do. Take an acorn for instance. Because you've often seen how it develops into a tree, you take it for granted. Yes, I have hidden a mighty oak tree inside an acorn. Just think of all the other things that you can see that you take for granted. For example, consider water changing into ice or steam, depending upon the temperature. Then think of the things that you take for granted that you can't see. You can punch numbers on a cellphone – which isn't connected to anything – and, in seconds, you can speak with someone on the other side of the world. You can't see your spirit and yet you wonder about the validity of the spiritual world. Have I got news for you! There are more things existing that you can't see than those you can see! I have limited your receptors—your sensors— but you are learning to see and understand the spiritual world. Gradually, at a pace you can grow with comfortably, I will show you new insights. I love your curiosity, your deep desire to know me better. Keep listening. I won't disappoint you.

Wanting to know more ...

Lord, I'm thinking I want to know you in greater depth but as I write I'm thinking it is a desire for feeling closer. Or is it something else? I'm now wondering if it is a desire to know more ... more about why everything exists and how it works. It's a really deep curiosity alongside wanting to know you more and more. I know I can go to the Bible where it speaks of different people in different times in different cultures. Lord, I want to talk with you in my own time and my own culture. Is that presumptuous of me, or arrogant?

No. I understand you want to know how to best live for me in your own time and culture. You're seeking the quick answers. You live in a world where instant gratification is sought. I can supply instant answers as well as answers that are so slow they take centuries to emerge. Sometimes it takes many generations before insights into my creation are understood. As new theories are born, they in turn give rise to even newer theories of creation's patterns. Absolutely everything is in a continually evolving process. Everything that exists gives rise to everything new that comes into existence. Even the apparent process of dying gives rise to a new form. Nothing is wasted. I have made it so. Miraculous inventions come from existing materials. Humankind is always inventing. So am I. My processes are always creative.

I think I'm getting out of my depth here. It seems like you can start from nothing when you are creating, whereas we have to start from something already existing that you created.

That's true. But don't forget music and art and thoughts and dance, let alone spiritual growth. Language, music, sound

and other forms of movement have spiritual aspects to them. Spirituality is a part of all creativity. The things people are passionate about involve their spirituality. It could be their work or their hobby. A person's spirituality is also involved in their relationships. It is when I am welcome in people's lives that the whole of their lives, as well as the spiritual aspects of their lives, are enriched. I realise it sounds so complex when first heard, and yet it is also simple. Think of it like breathing. Most of the time you're not even aware that you are breathing, it is so simple to do. However, once you stop breathing you are very quickly aware of the lack of oxygen. Knowing me spiritually, walking beside me, thinking your thoughts with me makes your life as it was created to be, having a sense of peace and fulfilment. Abandon me and you will be aware that something is absent.

You've brought to mind a time when I felt that absence.

Are you thinking of the day you were standing at the sink washing the breakfast dishes?

Yes, I was. I had two little children under two years of age and my husband travelled away from home for his work. I found it so hard. He got the travelling job the same week I came home with the second baby. That day I was standing at the sink feeling unhappy. I was trying to identify why I was unhappy. I loved my husband and my children, but something elusive was missing. Your words of comfort came into my mind: 'Come unto me, all ye who labour and are heavy laden and I will give you rest.' I stood there and thought, I feel as if I labour, and I'm feeling heavy laden. But now I know what I am missing. I am missing you, Lord. I have become so busy I have stopped praying. I've stopped going to church. I've stopped worshipping you. I have to do something about this. It was a turning point in my life.

So what did you do?

So I talked with my husband and explained how I was feeling. He had a responsibility at the 9.30 am Sunday service at our church. We decided I would go to the 7.30 am service and he would mind the children. Then I would arrive home in time for him to attend the 9.30 am service. That way we could each attend communion, something we individually felt was important in our lives.

So what happened as a result?

I don't remember. I know that's what we did, and I recovered the missing bit in my life that had meant so much to me.

What was the missing bit?

It was worshipping you and partaking in communion. I don't know how to explain what happens. Something is fed in me that I need in order to be fully me. It is indefinable. It is intangible, and yet it is somehow totally wholesome.

You have done well to recall a moment that happened forty-six years ago.

I think of it as a God-given moment, a time when your Holy Spirit touched my thoughts.

You could be right.

Our conversation had come to an end. I welcomed the mists of sleep as I turned out the light.

Drawn to the garden ...

Here I am again. In a way it has been a sad day. Anyway, that is how I have felt. I attended Gaye's mother's funeral today and felt sad for Gaye and her family as they farewelled a wonderful woman. They are a real family of faith who love you very much. As Gaye was walking behind the hearse for the final farewell, holding on to her grandchild's hand I heard her say, 'You'll see her again, one day,' quickly adding, 'but not too soon.' So honest, so hopeful and, to my ear, with humour. However, I digress. Sadness stayed with me. Later, I got into the garden as the weeds needed attention. I was hoping to spend some quiet time with you and to lose my sadness. Why is it that gardening restores me in some way?

I have made it so. When you get down to the earth you are in touch with my creation. From earth you come, to earth you return. In a way you are touching base with the home of your earthly existence. If you are thinking of me at the same time it adds to the 'homewardness' of you and creation. I enjoy seeing you create beauty by allowing nature to move forward.

It seems to me like earth and death and life are all intertwined. Thank you for being with me this afternoon.

I knew you wanted to just be with me. Remember the Garden of Eden? It was in the garden that I talked with Adam and Eve. Perhaps now you'll understand why your seeking me, to just be with me, instinctively draws you to the garden.

Oh, Lord. Somehow you throw light on the obvious that I know but haven't seen!

Softly, softly as falling rain ...

Softly, softly, as falling rain
comes my love to ease your pain.
Where you've never been before
has opened like an open door.

A glimpse of me you now have seen
my depth of love has always been
behind a screen your eyes can't view
yet always there, surrounding you.

You choose to walk within this field
when unto me your heart you yield.
The arms which I outstretched before
enfold you now, and you adore.

Atonement and being in at-one-ment ...

I've just gone back through my journal and discovered it has been nearly six months since I first started chatting with you about the meaning of atonement. I don't think I'll ever forget during our first discussion on the subject, how you impressed upon my mind and heart the importance of understanding atonement. Shall I share what I did and said at the time?

Why not? I felt you got an insight that was meaningful to you.

Well, I certainly shared my uncertainties with you. As always, you take my straight talking and my questioning and seem to understand where I am coming from. I've reread it and think what I said could have been been expressed more gently. However, I realise that I wanted to uncover some of the teachings and understandings about atonement that did not sit easily with me. Fortunately, you know me and see into my heart. I'm really grateful that I can express my thoughts and my feelings so openly with you, and you understand where I am coming from.

My journal entry went like this:

'I've often heard Christians say that Christ died on the cross because God needed the blood of his son as a sacrifice in order to forgive humankind their sins—like a scapegoat! Is this the heart of the God that I want to call my God? I don't think so! You told the story of the prodigal son and the forgiving father. That father is more like my kind of God, a God with a heart of unconditional love.'

Following that entry, I looked up Young's Analytical Concordance to the Bible to find out what the New Testament said about atonement.

Saint Paul, in his letter to the Romans, spoke of reconciliation as the meaning ... I warmed to that. All the other references were to the Old Testament and seemed to talk about covering. I needed to know more. So guess what? I went to Google. It was there I discovered that over the centuries theologians had come up with a variety of theories about the meaning of atonement as they understood it had been achieved through the death of Christ.

I FOUND THE FOLLOWING HELPFUL TO MY THINKING:

- **God didn't need the death of Jesus. We needed it to show us how much he loved us and was prepared to sacrifice in order to show it.**

- **The apartness between Adam and God was turned around to at-one-ment and was shown through the death and resurrection of Jesus.**

- **Death, unleashed through Adam, was reversed in the resurrection of Jesus.**

I found it important to my thinking that Jesus told us he lay down his life of his own accord (John 10:18).
Finally, I went to where I should have started—seeking the Holy Spirit for wisdom about the meaning and significance of atonement. Mentally, I imagined walking along the water's edge with Jesus. Suddenly, he walked in front of me, abruptly turned, and we stopped. We met forehead to forehead, with me thinking, 'I want to understand the meaning of atonement. For me, it is about you showing your love for us.'

Immediately, I melted into insignificance. I disappeared. I was no more. In my place the globe of the earth was at the forehead of Jesus and I was like a pixel contained within that globe.

What struck me was that Jesus wanted the world to understand the meaning of at-one-ment. Not just me!

Thank you for going through that again. So how do you feel now after having thought about this for six months?

When I break up the word atonement into at-one-ment it is meaningful to my heart. I find it easier to understand that everything you did for us on the cross, as well as what you do for us all the time, is in order for us to be at-one with you. I think you really want us to know you and understand how much you love us. Am I right in thinking your sacrificial atonement was your way of showing us how much you wanted us to relate in an at-one-ment relationship with you?

Yes, you are. I deeply desire to be in relationship with each and every one of you. To sacrifice myself in order to give humankind this message was how it had to be. Why? So that the ultimate giving of myself and my lifeblood would show my dearly beloved creation that I was prepared to empty myself totally – to give everything of I AM with nothing held back. The Jesus of my godliness was prepared to do this for me. I know it sounds amazing to you. My Holy Spirit is also of my godliness and is part of the at-one-ment.

Lord, my at-one-ment with you is like a dance. There are times when I relate to the Jesus Christ of your godliness. Other times I'm chatting away to the Holy Spirit of your godliness. Believe it or not, there are times I am going direct to the God-part of your godliness. The funny thing is that I always feel I am relating to the totality of you. Am I being silly thinking like this?

Not at all. Whichever way you choose is fine with me. When your heart is open to my heart we are at one. You don't even have to

define which part of my godliness you are relating to. I know your heart and as long as you are open to me, my heart listens. You realise that my heart is the source of my love, just as your heart is the source of your love, don't you?

You blow me away. The depth of your love and your willingness to be at-one with us is the greatest gift you can possibly give. I understand also, that is how you want us to be with each other here on earth. If we were at-one with you, as well as at-one with each other, what a wonderful existence our earthly lives would be. It would be just as the Jesus of you prayed, 'Thy will be done on earth as it is in heaven.' So that's part of what it is like in heaven: communicative, loving, harmonious at-one-ment with you and with each other? No wonder we need an earthly experience. There is so much we have to learn and to practise. Humankind surely falls short when it comes to communicative, loving, harmonious relationships.

Yes. The human race has a way to go. To practise at-one-ment with me is an excellent place to start. When people are in relationship with me and not trying to be religious, duty-bound, correct or judgemental then they find they become harmoniously connected with others. What do you think of that?

You make it sound simple ... and it is simple if our hearts are in the right place. However, as a human race we seem to find it horrendously difficult.

It's the letting go of self in order to be with me and with others that's the first step. My Holy Spirit will do the rest.

So to take that first step should be our prayer and earnest desire?

Yes. It should.

At-one-ment is the essence of being ...

Being at-one with you is a very interesting process. If I try to explain it I find it's a bit like trying to hold onto something slippery. It's not that you move. It's that I loosen my grip, as it were. And you let me. I am totally free.

True. You are always free to be at-one with yourself. How would you define the difference between being at-one with me and being at-one with yourself?

You really ask the difficult questions of me. I guess you want me to dig deeper in order to uncover something important for me to understand.

You're right. Start digging.

Well, when I'm in at-one-ment with you I am listening to you. It's a bit like waiting for your guidance. I find the quiet thoughts that come into my mind are frequently of a challenging nature.

You're right. Sometimes there's something you need to work on in order for our closeness to increase. So how would you explain what happens?

I think of it as a bit like being obedient to you. If I follow your guidance there is often an unexpected, positive outcome. It's usually about something I shouldn't neglect, or something I should look deeper into, in order to see where I'm out-of-tune in my thinking, attitude or behaviour with you or with others.

It's not always comfortable for you when I nudge you, is it?

No, it's not. Sometimes I get a new perspective on a situation and there's an obvious solution that would never have crossed my mind in a million years. It takes courage to take the first step. If I keep focussed on the end result you have shown me, I find doors open miraculously. There is a sense of wonderment at each step of the way. Other times I hesitate. I don't want to take the step you are suggesting. You're still there, but I know the at-one-ment will be deeper if I follow your suggestion.

Is it worthwhile, this at-one-ment with me?

Lord, that's the ultimate question in life. You have just posed the most challenging question which covers two questions we humans often ask. However, we use different words.

Really? What questions are those?

Do you really exist and do we want to believe in you?

I want to know your answer so others may hear your voice.

There is no hesitation in my answer. At-one-ment with you is the essence of my being. Somehow it fills in something that is missing in the realm of all that I experience in life that is 'seen'. To me, you make sense of both the seen and unseen dimensions of my life. There is an added harmony to the reason for being. There is a sense of fulfilment in at-one-ment with you that maintains hope in all things. I have a foundation that is solid and I experience a deep peace. I relax in the knowledge that my search for the reason of existence has been answered.

You trust a lot in your at-one-ment, don't you?

Yes, I do. I believe it is the result of trusting in you.

You may well be right.

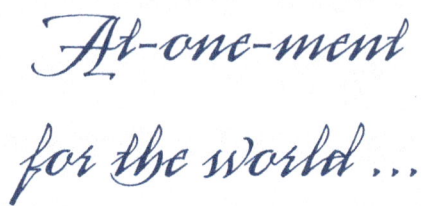

At-one-ment for the world...

I know you have other insights about 'at-one-ment'. Do you mind sharing them?

It's huge, Lord. For those who find it most comfortable to live in an extremely conservative container of faith, which has been asserted by many churches throughout the centuries, I would be seen as being outside the container. Many believe there is a God but, because of historical hurts suffered from churches, they want to have nothing to do with a church. However, what I think may bring them a sense of relief if they are searching for God.

You're side-stepping. Answer the question I asked you.

You're right. I am side-stepping. I realise there are so many folk who don't want to hear this.

So tell it for the people who do. I had the same trouble, you know.

Well, here it is. I think you wanted at-one-ment for the whole world. You made the way of at-one-ment possible for everyone who, in their heart, seeks to know God.

You're not saying anything new. I said and did that pretty clearly.

Yes. I know. Well, here goes. People who say you are the only way to be in at-one-ment with God are accused of being arrogant. It's as if they say that being a Christian is the only way of being at-one with the God of your godliness. I think it is a bit different to that.

I think of a bridge between humankind and God. I think you built the bridge – and you are the bridge. You, the bridge, with the help of the Holy Spirit, enable all true searchers of every God-seeking religion to have at-one-ness with the facets of God that God chooses to make available to them while meeting their culture and their time. I perceive that God wants all facets of the God-self to ultimately be available to all for relationship. I see this as being God's business and not mine. However, I may be wrong. To sum up, I think you taught us firstly that God loves us and wants each of us to experience at-one-ment. But there's more than that. God wants the world's people to experience at-one-ment with each other and understand that what you did in atonement, you did for everyone, if they wish to avail themselves of being at one with God. Also, I see richness in each dimension of faith in God and we have much to learn from one another.

Next day ...

I have reread what I wrote yesterday as overnight I felt concerned that what I had written was of me and may not have been of you.

Stop there! You answered me honestly from your own point of view. That is what I asked you to do!

Lord, I don't want to be out of step with you.

I realise that. Read what you wrote a second time and come back to me. I have some things I want to share with you.

Follow your own calling ...

Your responsibility is to share with others the chats we have. I am talking to the heart of you, and you are talking to the heart of me. I meet everyone where they are when they seek me or respond to the prompts of my Holy Spirit. You do not have to convert people or answer to others who want to restrict you in religious straitjackets. Your ability to chat with me is what I desire for every member of the human race. I am not looking for right or wrong. I am looking at hearts and their earnest desire to chat with me in their own relationship with me. I can guide them.

I left only two commandments. Love your God with all your heart, your mind and your strength. The second commandment was to love your neighbour as yourself. If everyone was doing that they would be busy listening whilst loving and caring for one another. Don't worry about people who search for me in another way or through another religion. That is my concern, not yours. I told you that in my Father's house there are many mansions. Who exists where is God's business. We can handle it. Humankind has developed so many prejudices, makes so many judgements, and promotes fear of one another instead of promoting loving, generous kindness. I'm really giving it to you straight.

I don't mind straight. Essentially you are telling me we each need to mind our own business and walk in an open, chatty, listening relationship with you and with each other. I think the reality is if we all did that we would be living a heavenly existence.

You've got it! But I also know you are not naive. Your thoughts are wandering into the areas of evil – things like genocide and wanton killing of others. Currently, the world is much troubled by this. It always has been. Nothing is new. However, humans have the ability to organise systems and structures if they are determined to really listen to one another and put a stop to such situations.

I sometimes wonder if wisdom is ever going to have a chance with the human race. Lives have been lost over land claims, slavery, racial differences, religious differences, emancipation, sexual orientation – the list goes on and on. Now many are arguing over who has the right to love whom.

You really have opened a can of worms, haven't you? Everything comes back to humankind loving God and loving one another.

Lord, it just seems too big for me to grasp. This can of worms seems enormous.

Don't try to solve the problems of the world. That is not your responsibility. You are asked to be at-one with me where you are. Believe me, enough will cross your path for you to respond to. So you are aware of the refugees in the world at the moment (I know that's what you are thinking of as a huge world problem). What are you doing to ensure there is a loving, inclusive welcome in your own community for refugees? Be a voice and an action where you are. I'm calling different people all over the world to pick up different responsibilities. Chat with me about the things you can do where you are, if that is

what I am laying on your heart. Listen to me and discern if I am calling you to encourage others to give of themselves in this area. Remember, at the moment I am calling you to write and publish your conversations with me. This is so others can come to know me in the same way. The more folk I have in at-one-ment with me, the more there is that can be achieved physically and spiritually.

OK. As usual you make it more practical and realistic. My mind automatically goes to the big picture that is bigger than I can handle. So it's back to reality for me, here and now, to get on with what you are calling me to do.

You've got it. Don't be so put off by the big problems of the world that you give up on the daily, bite-sized pieces that I require of you.

Thank you for reminding me. I want to think about all this. I'm going outside to look at a wonderfully stunning stretch of the sea – not an imaginary one, but a real one. In my heart and mind I will take these things with us as I worship you in the beauty of your creation.

So I left for the beach and later returned to the quiet of the night thinking about where I was being called to be.

From the edge of the beach ...

From the edge of the beach, I surveyed the sea
the wonder of you beside a sand's grain of me.
The moment we shared had no sense of time,
to be with you was just sublime.
My heart was moved by the beauty I'd seen
in nature's own evolving screen.

Creation really is your art,
it's love's ignition from the start.

You touch our lives where we each stand
we blindly tread upon your land.
We need to treasure one another
by ceasing war and then uncover
the world is ours to share with you.
Could we really start anew?

At-one-ment
in simplicity ...

Jesus, the other night I was in the quiet place that enfolds you within my heart and mind. There I was, just thinking about you and loving you. A picture of you on the cross came into my mind and I found myself mentally moving forward to enfold your feet in my arms. My love was just pouring out to you and tears were flowing, washing your feet, as my hair, which had become long, was moving in the breeze to dry them away. What a powerful moment of love it was. It seemed to me that you bent down and enfolded me with your arms. That was impossible, Lord. Somehow with your mind, in the midst of your agony, you were able to let me feel your loving arms. What an incredible experience that was.

From that night on, I have been able to embrace your feet at the cross during quiet moments when I have thought of my love for you.

Then came the night when once again I visualised being at the foot of the cross, enfolding your broken feet close to my heart. You seemed to say to me,

Come higher. It is heart to heart I want you to be with me.

Don't ask me how it was achieved ... but there I was placing my arms of love around your broken body. Slowly, I disappeared ... melting into you. It was a moment of at-one-ment.

I have no other words to describe it. I just feel incredibly humbled to have had such an experience.

Your love for me is important to me. I wanted to show you what at-one-ment is like.

I truly have no words for it. It is such an amazing place to be. The peace and the sense of belonging are incredible. In the Old Testament scriptures God tells us he has carved a place for us in the palm of his hand. I now understand, Jesus, that you carved a place for us in the heart of your heart. It is the place of refuge where we can rest, trusting in you eternally.

I am always there for you and for those who seek me.

How could I not have shared this experience with you, the reader?

If I hadn't, it would have been lost …

                    it would have been lost.

Stronger for having been weak ...

I have been wondering what our next conversation would be about. This morning during communion I felt I received some direction. It seemed as if you were nudging me to tell about the time I had hepatitis.

I did give you a nudge. That was a huge learning time in your life, wasn't it?

Yes, it was. I recall we had just sold our home and bought a business. We moved into a house alongside the business for six months. Then the week before I fell sick we moved into yet another home which we rented. New schools had to be found as we tried to settle again. Our younger son was about to turn five. There were seventeen months between the two boys and we were hoping to bring some stability into our lives after a pretty chaotic time of change. Drunken street parties had interrupted our Saturday evenings and we had feared for our safety. Hence the second move.

It was an extremely busy and stressful time for you, wasn't it?

It was. At the time, I couldn't understand why I felt so unwell. To cut a long story short, I had hepatitis. For two months I felt deeply seasick and then for a few days I seemed to recover. Unfortunately, I relapsed and the process started all over again ... only I felt even worse. The day came when I was sent to hospital by ambulance. For six weeks I was on a drip. The sensation of deep seasickness stayed with me continuously, hour after hour, week in and week out. The only time I was not aware of it was when I was asleep. However, I think you gave me a miracle in the midst of the six weeks. I've always thought it was you. Am I correct?

Tell me what happened and why you thought it was me.

It was Anzac Day in 1974. I'll never forget it. The hospital chaplain came to give me communion. For ten minutes after receiving communion I was free of the nausea and I could hardly believe it. It was like a promise, a taste of getting better, an encouragement to hope that I would get better.

And did you?

Yes, I did. I was discharged from hospital the day before my thirtieth birthday. It took me two years to make a full recovery. For months I never knew what each day would bring. Would I feel well enough to get up and get dressed? I remember the first day I got into the car to drive up the road. What a day that was. It felt so strange to be doing such a normal thing after so many months of forced acceptance of an extremely quiet and careful life.

What else did you learn during that time?

I learnt to let go and take each day one at a time. I held onto the promise I perceived when I was in that ten minutes of not feeling sick.

Turning thirty wasn't a problem. I was so glad to be alive that I welcomed being thirty instead of feeling sad at leaving my twenties. I was glad to be alive for my husband and my children. I was grateful for friends who looked after our boys after school each day and for those who had them during the holidays.
We had one woman who came and cleaned for us and another woman who prepared the evening meal and oversaw the children's

evening bath. I was so dependent upon the care of others. How fortunate we were to have the help of those folk!

So after your experience of such helplessness what learning emerged for you?

I discovered I was stronger for having been weak. That having learnt to let go of so much I was actually stronger in me. Perhaps it came from understanding that at my weakest point you met me and carried me through.

It's not the only time in your life that you've found me at a very weak point, is it?

No, Lord. It's not. Perhaps that's why I feel led to share our journey with others.

You realise that it is in the darkest times that many folk find me, don't you? I am always there. My touch is frequently recognised when folk later look back to a turning point in their lives. Other times, I am there beside them and they never know it. There are times when I welcome them through from earth to eternity. You came close to death but it wasn't your time. There was still much for you to experience and to share. That was part of your journey.

Gifts singular and merging...

Today I found myself in a discussion with some friends who also believe in you. We were trying to make sense of why sometimes people are miraculously healed, yet at other times folk aren't healed. We were talking about physical healings.

I know. I was listening. It was interesting that it was mainly physical healings you were talking about. Do you remember discussing emotional, mental or spiritual healings?

No. I don't. The closest we got to spiritual healings was talking about naming and casting out demons. I'm out of my depth there. It's not that I think those things don't exist. It's just that I think when I'm focussed on you in my life I don't even have to think about them. In other words I don't want to give them the power or the satisfaction of recognition. They are to have no place in my life. I'm most likely naive in this area as it is written that you cast out demons. However, I think it comes under the area of a special gifting – a ministry which you give to a few – but, as in all ministries, if we are focussed on you it is actually you and your Holy Spirit doing the work. By grace, you work through individuals with the ministry you have allocated to each one.

In many ways you are right. Saint Paul told how each of the gifts, when brought together, edified the body of Christ. It is simple and yet it is also complex. It comes back to you being in relationship with me. If you are listening to me, and find yourself being called upon to respond to someone's particular need, then listen for my guidance. It will give you the right insight. You call it discernment. However, you need to be sure you are hearing me through both your heart and your head together ... and not just hearing what you think you want to hear.

It's very tricky. This is an area that can be subtly invaded by negative forces. Your relationship with me needs to be pure and uncluttered. Am I making sense to you?

I think so. In essence I've understood I'm not to dabble in these things. It needs to be abundantly clear that where I am coming from is (a) biblical, (b) recognised by others, and (c) comes from a direct, loving relationship with you. Somewhere, mixed up in all of this, is to be a total lack of personal pride and not wanting to be seen as a 'spiritual guru'. Seeking recognition or status are sure signs of not being in tune with you.

True. I know when the time is right to introduce a particular gifting into a person's life. Sometimes it develops over a number of years. That's mainly what happened for you. However, sometimes I work instantaneously. You have experienced both. Remember the night I woke you. I knew I needed to do that otherwise you never would have picked up a pen and started this journey of writing. Am I correct?

Yes, you are. It never would have occurred to me to pick up a pen and write for pleasure – let alone write a book. To me, writing has always been a discipline. Even when I send someone a birthday card I write the message on a piece of paper first to check it makes sense. When I'm writing for you it usually just flows. Is that one of the reasons why I still feel bemused by this process of writing like this?

Yes, it is. Because you are aware of your own weakness you are also aware of my strength. I have enabled you to do something that you recognise is not totally of you. You recognise me in the process. It is that recognition of me in the process of any gifting that allows the gift to flow. Gradually, trust grows to the point of confidently undertaking a process of gifting from me that

becomes a ministry. Sometimes multiple gifts merge to enrich an individual's ministry. The key is living in your at-one-ment with me while listening to and obeying my nudges. Am I making sense to you?

Yes, you are. When I look back over my life I can see a sequence of events which were preparing me for where I am at the moment. It was important that I stepped out in faith in order to grow through the challenges that often felt daunting.

Do you now understand why different people have different gifts and no one has all the gifts?

Yes, I do. Saint Paul gave us the message pretty clearly when he told us the Holy Spirit gives a different gift to each person. That way we each have a place and are equally valued in our differences. We need one another as we minister in your name. You are the source of our bonding. So when I go back to my ponderings about healing, you have used our discussion to show me some answers through my journey in writing. Have I understood you correctly?

If this has answered your questions then I have spoken to you in a way you understand. If I was answering someone else I would speak through their lives and their experiences to bring them to a point of understanding. In your world of education today, you would call it teaching.

Yes. You have just brought an insight into yesterday's reflections which makes sense to me. I smile. My profession was in education and you have used a process I recognise. You really are the ultimate teacher.

Now, I'm smiling.

All is contained in whoever ...

The other week I was talking with you about at-one-ment for all. You came and showed us how much you loved us because you wanted us to understand that your desire was for us to meet you heart-to-heart in relationship. Have I understood that correctly?

Yes, you have. You understood the cross was my way of showing everyone that I loved humankind deeply. It also showed I was prepared to relinquish everything. I was prepared to die to self so you could see through my dying to my resurrection. I had overcome the death put on Adam and his descendants. My resurrection was the new promise. There was even more to come. The Holy Spirit was sent to encourage and empower all who follow me.

Lord, I want to ask you about the 'all'. In John 3:16 you said whoever believes in you would have everlasting life. You said, 'whoever'. That means 'all' who believe in you, doesn't it?

Yes it does. All means all. I don't cast aside any person of any ethnicity, creed or sexual orientation. I include every human being on the earth who turns to me and believes in me. Do you consider me heartless? My message was to show I died so all may know my love is for each and every one of them: the sinner, the prisoner, the poor, the young, the old, the downtrodden, those who are different or cast out by society, the sick, the contagious, ethnic minorities—the list goes on and on—and it includes all. 'Whoever' is contained in 'all' and 'all' is contained in 'whoever'. Have I made myself clear?

Yes, Lord. Abundantly clear. So many times throughout history we seem to have heard only what we wanted to hear.

You're right. There has been a huge history of misinterpretation of what I said and did. When you go back over the centuries you find people have used politics, power and wealth to manipulate my church and my people. People are now able to read my word and see there are many layers and depths to my words to be uncovered. My Holy Spirit is a wonderful director and teacher for those who genuinely seek what I said, and not what they hope I said. Your searching of Scripture is unfolding things for you, isn't it?

Yes, it is. I seem to be always learning more about you.

An Easter Sunday conversation ...

Today is such a special day. My thoughts and prayers are of deep thankfulness for what you went through to show us how much you love us ... and then how you came back to show us that death and separation from God had been overcome. Here we are, millions of us, celebrating around the world over 2,000 years later. How amazing is that!

So what were your reflections today?

I thought of how out of every sorrow, every grief and every negative thing that exists there is the opportunity for something positive to emerge. It seems God has programmed such a process if we are prepared to look for it and engage with him.

Can you think of a time when something negative happened to you that you were able to be thankful for later in life?

Yes, I can. When I had hepatitis it never occurred to me that I would ever be grateful for the experience ... but the day came when I was.

What happened?

It was when my first husband was diagnosed with bowel and liver cancer. As a result of knowing how ill he was feeling in his final weeks, I was able to better care for him because of that understanding. I found myself giving thanks that I had experienced a very sick liver.

Are there other occasions where you see new growth emerge due to tragic circumstances?

Yes there are. If I look back over my life I discover that out of my weakest moments my greatest strengths have emerged. Other times when a door has seemed to close another has opened. Sometimes, I have stepped out expecting to meet what I thought would be impossible challenges. To my amazement I have been able to achieve what seemed impossible outcomes. When I have failed at something there has been an important lesson for me to discover.

So what is the outcome of all of this for you?

At some depth I carry hope. I observe what is happening around me and expect the possibility of good outcomes. Sometimes an expectation contains responsibility and action. Sometimes it doesn't. Having you present in my life makes a difference. I discern a guidance and wisdom that I can choose to listen to. You even leave me free to follow or not follow such nudges. It certainly makes for a very interesting life.

So my death and resurrection encourages you to carry hope in your life on an everyday basis. Is this what you are trying to tell me?

Yes, it is. I'm not always great at it, but when I look back I often see a bigger picture that shows me new growth and new opportunities. It's really worth reflecting sometimes ... just to see how you create such things at such a personal level.

It's not just a personal level, you know. It's also at every level you can think of ... even at a worldly or a cosmic level.

I think I've discovered that, Lord. It's at a cellular level, too. Actually it goes from the infinitely small to the infinitely large, neither of which we can humanly measure. We try, but we're still learning.

That's true. I'm glad you can see all this. However, I'm also glad you understand my desire to be at one with humanity and that my resurrection has birthed hope.

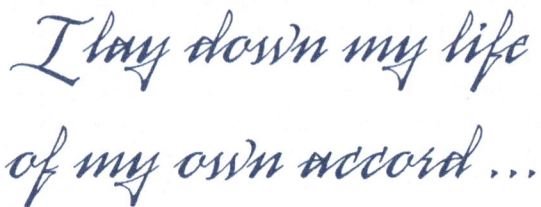

I lay down my life of my own accord...

You have been thinking about sacrifice lately. I discern that you want to understand why I allowed myself to sacrifice my life. More to the point – did God demand it of me?

Yes, Lord. It is something I've always wondered about. Easter reminds me of how hard I find it to reconcile a loving God requiring the suffering and death of his son. I can't quite believe he required you to suffer for all the sins of humankind. It just doesn't make sense to me.

First of all, nothing God does has to make sense to you. However, have you ever considered that maybe I wanted to put an end to sacrifice? You saw how I reacted to the moneylenders in the courts of the Temple. I was really angry at how sacrifices were being adulterated in the courts of a holy place. Sacrifices were being made as a duty. People were coming to worship out of duty and fear, not out of love for their heavenly father. On top of that, greed and extortion were rife.

So you wanted people to come to know God as a God of love, and not as a God of law and legality? Did you realise you were trying to change people's whole way of thinking and behaving. It takes something pretty dramatic to change anyone's understanding of how to meet the requirements of their God.

I knew whatever I did would have to capture the hearts and the minds of the human race. Therefore it would have to take my all. In order for people to understand how much God loved them I would have to give my total self and the only way to show that was to give my life.

So God didn't demand the sacrifice of your life? You offered your life to show us how much you and he loved us and he honoured that and revealed his love for you and for us in your resurrection. Things are now starting to make sense to me. Now I know why John 10:18 jumped out of the page at me. It is where it is recorded that you said you laid down your life of your own accord.

You're beginning to grasp the significance of those words. I can see you have been trying to understand many things about my death and resurrection. You have also pondered for years about sacrifice and where it fitted with God's expectations of me and the giving of my life. Now you are seeing it as my gift of love to humankind so that each may understand they have a loving father and not a punishing, fearsome ogre for their God. He loves me so much he resurrected me, even though humans killed me. I showed my resurrected self to reveal that His love and power could overcome death. Yes, you're starting to see it. What do you think now?

Think! I am just so grateful that my search has led me to where I am not disappointed. It is so comforting to know that I can come to you with my questions and somehow you know how to speak to me in a way that honours my concerns. I just couldn't believe that God would demand you to be a scapegoat for us. I can believe that you were prepared to offer yourself in order to show us how loving your dynamic trinity is. I'm glad your Holy Spirit enables the 'me of me' to communicate with the 'you of you'. Alleluia!

Wealth that disturbs me: a paradox emerges ...

Lord, tonight I watched a documentary on the history of the Eastern Orthodox church. What that church has been through and how it has survived is mind-boggling. Despite the persecution and the attempts to obliterate belief in you, the hearts of the people have been able to carry you with them through the centuries.

Yes, in spite of all those attempts, my spirit can live and be kept alive in the hearts of those who look to find me. You have another overview that disturbs you that you are pondering upon. You're trying to grasp it with your mind and your heart. Do you mind sharing it here?

It's the pomp and ceremony of so many churches that disturbs me. The distance between the humbleness of your life and the richness of church vestments, icons and ceremony brings a discord to my heart. Can you make sense of any of this for me?

I don't know if I will make sense for you. Be careful of judging. Most rituals and ceremonies are expressions of honouring me, God the Father and the Holy Spirit. In their richness of spending an earthly price they are outward signs showing respect to our Godliness! Carried within is a tradition embodying worship which can be encapsulated by the intangible, spiritual, ethnic expression of the people.

I can see that. I'm getting a glimpse of understanding.

You have just got an even deeper understanding which has flashed through your mind. You have been thinking of what has been spent on such things when there is so much poverty in

the world. Suddenly you understood another dimension. See if you can uncover it in words.

I suddenly thought of the amount of money that was poured into warfare and destruction. The amount of money that has been spent in trying to express honour to God is a drop in the ocean compared with what is being and has been spent on warfare. I should be more concerned about that. However, both lots of spending keep the poor in their state of poverty and the powerless in their hovels. You showed us in the simplicity of your life that we have got it wrong in both areas – but one is much worse than the other. Now I find myself making a judgement. You warned me about judging at the beginning of this conversation.

Yes, I did.

Could a solution be to stop spending money in both areas? No more rules, regulations and outward paraphernalia in the church alongside no more spending on warfare. Just think of what could be done if humankind focussed on creating a better environment instead of focussing on destruction.

I agree. However, the hearts and minds of everyone would have to be in agreement. I came and showed how that could be achieved. It is in finding at-one-ment with me that heaven on earth can be realised. Mother Teresa, Desmond Tutu, Mahatma Gandhi, St Francis, Dietrich Bonhoeffer and many others have shown the world what my life was about. While money and power are worshipped you will always have corruption. When corruption rules you will always have war. Where does that leave your thinking now?

Feeling extremely helpless, Lord. The only person I can influence is me. I need to be your little bit of salt where I am. I've come to a better understanding of rituals carrying folk through the generations. I can see how the outward expressions of honouring you have enabled hearts throughout the centuries to honour you. I find myself more disturbed about the distribution of the plenty you have given us being destroyed by greed and warfare. I'm just so surprised you haven't given up on all of us in our communal sin.

I covered that on the cross. I showed you my love for humankind was greater than any sins the world of humans could create. You are not forsaken.

Marvelling but not necessarily recognising ...

It's about six weeks since I last felt the nudge to write. Much thinking has ensued. Life situations, conversations and books I have read have been dancing through my mind, interweaving steps that bring enlightenment and questioning alongside each other. Always at the baseline, like the underlying rhythm of a piece of complex music, there has been the richness of the understanding of at-one-ment. You really meant me to look into at-one-ment from many angles, didn't you?

Yes, I did. I want you to discover the depths of what at-one-ment with me means. There are many insights and layers to what my 'atonement' means for humankind. Some won't emerge for you until your spirit has moved on from its earthly existence.

Is that why you gave me a quick glimpse in my mind of a heavenly host at-one with you and God? I didn't so much see God as have an awareness of the presence of light and of me being a part of the host ... just like being a pixel in a screen.

Yes. It was a quick glimpse, wasn't it? I'm glad you perceived it and pondered on it. I wanted you to know at-one-ment goes on forever and each and every one of you is a part of it.

I feel the baseline of our existence is at-one-ment with you and our time here is to discover this. Am I getting it right?

You already know the answer to that. At-one-ment with me is at the heart of your walk in life. It is available to everyone. It can be experienced in many different ways and places. Each person can choose to see the miracle of me each day of his or her life.

It is when they stop and marvel in the depth of their being at the miracle of an aspect of life that is before them, that my spirit is able to touch their spirit with a flash of recognition and at-one-ment.

So humankind can marvel but not necessarily recognise what is happening in their spirit. Am I getting a glimpse of how you get overlooked?

Yes. It takes the sharing of spiritual awareness by those who are aware of my Holy Spirit in their life's journey which awakens awareness of me when daily miracles are observed.

There are so many layers to understanding at-one-ment and to marvel at you. I know I can only grasp a bit at a time. I appreciate your teaching having layers to it.

You realise that was why I taught in parables, don't you? There is always more to be uncovered when a parable is reflected upon. Also, my parables are timeless. They could be understood at the time by the ordinary people. Future scholars could educate listeners by giving the historic setting for each parable. However, those parables can also uncover truths in the midst of many cultural settings. They were not stories to be buried in the sands of time. They were to speak to folk of any day and age. Do you understand what I am saying?

I think so. The stories you told held timeless truths which could be discovered by listeners or readers in any century. As we rehear them they bring fresh insights if we ask you to further enlighten us as we think about them. Your Holy Spirit surely touches the hearts and minds of genuine searchers. Don't you ever get tired with our slowness to understand?

No. Never. The honest enquiries of those who seek are a source of great delight. The journey for all humankind is to seek the heart of me – to discover the joy and peace of being at-one with me. Yes, it is a journey. It is a journey embarked upon with free will. People choose whether they will search for me or whether they will ignore the nudges that stir them to seek for the reason for being. Have you thought about that?

Many a time. It is so easy in this day and age to think we are intellectually superior and don't need to acknowledge the quiet, unobtrusiveness of our spirituality. Education has been a blessing. However, it has also invoked our pride into ignoring what we can't prove. Science has been a blessing also. Initially, humankind thought science was at odds with spirituality. I'm thinking that as scientific knowledge has expanded the so-called gap between science and spirituality has diminished. What do you think about that?

You could be right. It depends what your scientists discover and how they interpret their discoveries. As I told you before, to date, there is more yet to be discovered than has already been discovered. There is more unseen than is seen ... the tiniest and the largest still exist in the world of the unknown or the unproven by humankind.

I'm not worried about that. We will learn about these things as we need to know them. What concerns me is how we will use each piece of knowledge we uncover. We still haven't learned how to love one another. As a whole human race we haven't learned how to be at-one with you or with each other. We use our knowledge to build as well as to destroy. Somehow, as humans, we seem to prefer to destroy rather than to create for the betterment of each other.

Why do you think so much remains hidden? You have opened another can of worms, haven't you? I'm pleased you have discerned how good it would be if everyone worked together for the benefit of humanity. I'm also aware you are disturbed by mankind's inhumanity to mankind.

Enough for today. Your mind and spirit need to rest. Come for one of your walks along the water's edge with me and let us be at-one in the silence. We started this conversation with at-one-ment. Let's finish it by being in at-one-ment.

Grief and loss can bring birth ...

I had been out one evening amongst a large group of women who had gathered to hear a guest speaker. During a quiet moment I suddenly knew that everyone present had lived through heart-breaking moments. Beneath the surface I could discern that resilience lay within the chatty friendliness of the women. I pondered upon this.

> Is it mainly in the bleak, heartbreaking moments of our lives that we can best find you? It seems to me many folk find you in times of crisis, challenge or heartache.

Many times it is a while after the initial shock or despair that I am found in stillness and quietness. Often it is after anger and verbal despair that I am heard in a quiet moment. What is heard is seldom the sound of my voice. It's a quiet thought ... or a moment of peace ... or a calm acceptance of a situation. I am discovered where I am not expected in the midst of a reality which has brought a tremendous change in a person's life.

> How does this experience of you impact on people's lives?

It can be totally dismissed or it can be gratefully received. It can even be experienced and not recognised as coming from me. I accept every kind of response. I give everyone the freedom to listen or not to listen ... to accept or not to accept ... to respond or not to respond. That's how it has to be when you are given free choice.

> It has struck me that most folk have experienced grief, loss, heartache or loneliness at some time in their lives. Do these serve as avenues to discover you, or is there more to it than that?

There is more. You are focussed on painful experiences of life at the moment. Would you appreciate joy, new birth, love and fellowship if you didn't know their opposites? Each highlight or crisis counterbalances its opposite so you can recognise each for what it is. Life would be very bland if it was monotonous. However, compassion, empathy, understanding and sympathy would also be non-existent. Can you see any positives within that reasoning?

Yes, I can. I also see it's where resilience is born, and how strength can emerge and inner peace can be discovered. Not only are our experiences multi-faceted but we are too.

So too am I multi-faceted … and you have been created in my own image. There's nothing you have experienced that I haven't experienced with you. That's why I came to earth. Our shared earthly experiences are yet another facet of our at-one-ment.

Powerlessness can birth strength ...

It was the middle of the night. I was quietly drifting in the place between being asleep and being awake. Slowly a thought collected its tendrils.

Have you ever had moments of feeling totally helpless?

I knew where that question came from. I was being nudged to write.

> You want me to recall the most vulnerable moments in my life, Lord. Really? And then you want me to write about them?

The silence was extremely silent.

I knew I was being called to another moment of obedience. However, I wanted to make sure I was hearing correctly. The moments of helplessness are the moments of deepest, earthly vulnerability.

> Lord, the moments of helplessness were the moments when I felt I had absolutely no control over situations in my life. They were moments of complete nakedness and vulnerability of my being. Are you really nudging me to share my moments of helplessness when I had not one minute element of control over what was happening ... the moments when physically, mentally and emotionally I met the edge of how far I could be stretched?

> **You already know what I am nudging you to write about. You are aware everyone has moments similar to yours. Tonight I'm suggesting you make the list of your powerless moments. You have come to an understanding about how your powerless moments have given birth to an insight upon which you rest. At this point in time, what is that insight?**

It's sort of simple and yet it's complex. It seems to me we are as but 'leaves in the breeze'. Just as the leaves of autumn are freely carried by the wind to their resting place, we too are carried by your Holy Spirit to ours. I've watched leaves dance as they are lifted to soar in a strong breeze. I've watched some species of leaves spin seemingly out of control, yet they're beautifully balanced as they make their descent to earth. Some just drop without much of a dance at all. I think I have discovered we can be like the leaves and you can be like the wind. As the leaves let go of their branches and trust the wind to carry them, so too can we let go of our sense of total control and trust you to be with us wherever we may go. There is a saying, 'Let go and let God'. It is such a simple concept but such a complex actuality to achieve.

It seems to work for you most of the time. Now you've had some time to think about it, are you prepared to list some of the helpless moments in your life?

Yes, I can list some of them. They will serve as a reminder of how I came to be thinking like this. Strangely enough, in thinking about them, I have discovered they were defining and pivotal moments in my life and faith. They were:

- the night I was in labour with my first child
- the weeks of ongoing nausea when I had hepatitis
- my husband dying in my arms
- my father dying in my arms
- the bus accident in Austria where five fellow passengers and the driver were killed
- the awareness of broken relationships due to religious differences

- my mother dying in my arms
- the ambulance trip when I considered the possibility of my own death
- discovering my younger son dead in his bed from a heart attack

Now I am intrigued. Through all these moments of powerlessness – these weakest moments of my life – I can see that the strength you gave me has emerged, developed and grown immeasurably. Within some of the experiences I have been instantaneously aware of you. Within others, I wasn't aware of your presence until a long time afterwards. However, I now know you were always there. It was me who was discovering the presence of you.

Your listing of these experiences has shown you that your moments of being most helpless are at the moments of birth and death. Can you word that understanding succinctly?

Yes. It is in the moments of birth and death we can find you. The finding can be instantaneous or it can emerge over a time of reflection – if we choose to look for you. Always there is choice. Out of birth comes the joy of celebrating a new life. Out of death, if your existence is accepted, there comes a sense of completeness. Once again there is a paradox. Perhaps that is the biggest lesson in life: there is always paradox and you are in the tension of it.

What a lot you are learning from your life experiences. There is more, you know.

I thought about where God can be found and the paradoxes kept emerging.

Where is it, this closeness to God? ...

Where is it ...
this closeness to God?
It is within ...
It's the totality of the 'I am' of me merged with the total 'I am' of God.
And how do I experience this closeness?
It is one, and yet it is multi-dimensional ...
having many faces.
It is when I think about breathing it ...
but it happens with every breath, thinking or not.
It is when I consider the beauty of a leaf ...
or the majesty of the universe.
It is in the marvel of birth ...
as well as the wholeness of death.
It is in my imagination ...
adjacent to my logic.
It eludes me ...
creeping up on me unannounced.
It is in the moments I love spontaneously ...
including the moments I find it difficult to love.
It is empty ...
whilst being all-pervasive.
It is in my going out ...
and in my coming in.
It is so deep and so high ...

I don't have to chase it ... I just have to be.

It's the eternity of me.

Silent yet loud attention-getters ...

I have reflected upon our last two discussions and your last words to me have become clearer. You meant you wanted me to share more. I hadn't finished. You want me to share how you use nature to reassure me of your spiritual existence. It is so ephemeral ... so slippery ... so unbelievable ... so open to scepticism ... and yet I recognise it easily as I walk with you. Non-believers in you will dismiss this. Those searching for you will find this extremely thought-provoking. Folk you are at-one with will recognise you have the ability to reveal your presence in very personal and touching ways through nature. Sceptics will dismiss it immediately. It will challenge their understanding to even consider you are a God who can communicate so personally through coincidences that are too coincidental to be coincidental. On the edge of the unbelievable you have shown me that you are believable. You did it in the resurrection of Jesus. That was a silent yet loud attention-getter. The things I'm thinking about are so minimal they can't be seen – except by the person you mean it for.

Once again you are seeing the paradoxes through which I am observable. You have seen the analogy between the infinitely large and the infinitely small dimensions within which I exist and operate. Humankind is exploring this in the physical by trying to understand the extremes of the universe alongside insights of nanotechnology. You have just mentioned the extremes of my spiritual revelation to the world through my resurrection and put it alongside my spiritual revelations to you at an intensely personal level of communication. Just as people can communicate with one another through subtle, silent body language, I can communicate with you through subtle, silent messages in nature.

You're reminding me of how you used a falcon to communicate with me, aren't you? You are nudging me to share my experience of a bird bringing me a message of reassurance from you.

It took you a while to get to this point. You have already recorded it elsewhere. How about finding it and inserting it here? It will explain what we have been talking about.

Okay, Lord. I'll see if I can find it.

You will. You won't need to explain what you wrote. Just include it as it is.

Lord, I found it. I had put it on Facebook just over a year ago. The bird wasn't a hawk and it wasn't an eagle; it looked more like a falcon to me so that's what I called it.

THIS IS WHAT I WROTE.

The following poem tells the story of an experience I had a year ago. My younger son had died a few months previously. He had been a computer programmer and absolutely adored eagles and falcons.

The number plate on his first car was EAGLE1. Further, he often used a password which included Falcon1 interlinked with other letters.
This particular experience saw me driving in the outback of New Zealand on a country road surrounded by bush. As often happens, one can come across a hawk feeding on roadkill. As a car approaches, these birds reluctantly lift off, soaring out of sight in a short space of time. Coincidence or not, these are the thoughts that came to me after I experienced being stopped in the middle of nowhere by a very bold bird. Does God send messages for us to see in the everyday things? Perhaps God does. Do we read messages in the everyday things? Perhaps we do.

The falcon stood...

The falcon stood – unmoved by me
claimed its ground as firm could be.
Its powerful eyes were linked to mine,
midst bleak weekend, was this a sign
sent by my son to let me know
his afterlife he could now show?

My car stopped still – just like the bird –
a transfixed second – just absurd.
The prey it found was then ignored
as to the skies it powerfully soared.
Surrounding bush a living screen,
a message sent I felt I'd seen.
Would this I trust as I moved on?
Son's password choice was Falcon One.

So did that experience talk to you?

You know it did. Out of the unknown the unexpected arrived for a fleeting glimpse.

I thought it would speak to you. I know your son thought so also.

You really have it down to a fine art, don't you? At the moment I think I'm recognising something like this from you, it eludes me. I want to grasp the experience and hold onto it, but like a wriggly fish it slips out of the grasp of my recognition and all I have left is a memory. When I stop to think about these moments I find there are many. I hadn't realised how many! Does everyone have moments like these?

Everyone does. Each person is met in individual ways which have the ability to touch them personally. However, many folk consider similar experiences a figment of their imagination, or choose to ignore them in case others judge them as insane. Fear is a very repressive factor. Trusting in my ability to know everyone personally opens up a whole new dimension to life's experiences. The scientists of the world are just becoming aware that humankind is both physical and spiritual.

Many people find it difficult to find you ...

Lord, I feel that some of the thoughts I have attributed to you will be at odds with the beliefs of some theologians who, over centuries, have given their lives to studying the Bible and the things you taught. I don't want to be a false prophet and lead people away from you. Have the insights I've shared stepped outside what you would want me to write?

I gave you words that would encourage those who find 'god-fearing' theology difficult. The words I gave you will invite searchers of your day to experience my presence. This was what I was all about. When people experience the Trinity of Me, there I am with them and they will know me.

God, many people find it difficult to find you. Does it have to be so hard to find you?

Just think of me and there I am. I am within your mind and your heart, listening and waiting for you to tune in to my still, quiet voice. I have given each of you enough time to have life. Some lives are shorter than others. Don't worry about the shortness of any life. None is too short to meet me. My love encompasses all life, even life that doesn't experience the usual birth process.

Are you trying to tell me of your loving acceptance of those lost to miscarriage, abortion and stillbirth?

My loving arms await all life and all possibility of life. Every cell of my creation is of me. Some return to me in a transcendental form sooner than others. It is humankind's understanding of death which gives birth to the pain of absence. My resurrection was meant to overcome that pain.

Are you telling me that when we experience grief, it is unnecessary?

In a way—yes. In a way—no. When you look at it from the overview of eternity, yes ... for you are reunited with me within eternity. When you look at it within your earthly experience of time, no! Jesus wept when those he loved died. I needed to experience what grief feels like through his experience of it. We all need to experience grief within our lives. It is a part of becoming whole.

Lord, I'm finding this extremely deep. There's a sense of every cell of life being grieved over when it dies.

True—but you've missed the point. Nothing dies; everything changes to a new form. Nothing is wasted in my creation. I have made it so. In a sense you could call it recycling. The vibrations of existence may change, but they still vibrate in a new form. So it is with the spiritual form of you. You translate from one form of existence to another. Is it starting to make sense to you?

A bit. I need to think about this. Physically it makes sense. Now I'm trying to make sense of emotion.

Your experience of emotions will give you an appreciation of the joy that awaits you when you are with me in the spiritual form. All of your experiences in life cover a range of extremes. Think of any emotion and there is an opposite. Think of any sensation and there is an opposite. Think of any measurement and there is an opposite.

So living life is similar to a rubber band – we experience the different tensions of existence?

It is a bit like that. You could say what I am brings a stability within the stretching process. Analogies help your understanding – but they only go so far. The human mind, on its own, can reason only so far. In your current existence you need to let go and trust me. Can you do that?

I think I have to, Lord. Trusting you is the only way to inner peace. I think of the words you gave me the other night, 'All will be well'. Trusting in that promise carries assurance and peace.

Love dissolves fear ...

What a busy few weeks it has been. It seems as though you have brought many things to my attention. My mind has encountered many new ideas through books and music. I have found myself absorbed by books of near death experiences. Friends and friends' children have died. There seems to have been a lot about death and the life hereafter. Each time I have been led back to you.

I remember when I was about eight years old and suddenly realised I hadn't existed on earth when all the history I was learning about had occurred. It was a moment of shock. When Napoleon existed, I didn't. However, it also brought a comfort. In my non-existence on earth there had been nothing detrimental for me that I was aware of. I've often thought of that moment of insight. You have everything in hand. My non-existence on earth before my birth is not a problem. You look after us before birth and after death. It is written.

You're right. I have got everything in hand. Your life is a learning process. The existence of all that is seen and unseen needs a growing-into experience. You've had a couple of insights in the last twenty-four hours. Do you feel like sharing them?

They were quite important insights for me. I seemed to stumble over them ... but I know I didn't. As usual, you had been preparing the way. I have always found it difficult to understand why we are told in Scripture to fear God. Why fear a God who loves us unconditionally? Somehow it doesn't make sense to me! I was reading Psalm 103 and there it was again: the instruction to fear God. Thank goodness there are annotations in my version of the Bible. I was directed to another Psalm where fear was defined as meaning trust and obey. That meaning made sense to me. We can be imprisoned by our language due to changes of meaning over time. It was so good to discover my understanding of God need not include trepidation, anticipated pain, rejection, worthlessness or abandonment. In this day and age fear seems to be at the root of our existence. Even our entertainment is often filled with gruesome, fear-filled suffering. Many are scared to the point where they fear experiencing fear. What an indictment on our existence when love has the ability to dissolve fear. You've no idea how affirmed I felt in my thinking about God when I discovered that definition of fear.

Silence reigned between us for some weeks. Not the silence of not talking or not being together. I mean the silence of not receiving a nudge to record. Then, softly over a few days, I felt that nudge to get out my pen. So there I was, quietly in readiness, wondering what was about to emerge.

Prayer is not duty-bound ...

It has been some weeks now since I felt pen was to go to paper. There has been a heap of reading, thinking and just being in your presence. The importance of my understanding of at-one-ment with you keeps resonating in my mind and in my heart. The other day I was talking with someone about prayer and Bible reading. Somehow, I find I can't relate to you out of a sense of duty. Something in me rebels when it comes to doing things out of duty. My spirit and my heart want to act from the springboard of love. Honesty and integrity are as deeply ingrained as the source of love in action. The other day, out of the blue,

THE FOLLOWING WORDS CAME INTO MY MIND:

> **Prayer is not duty-bound**
> **It is love-bound.**
> **Surrender to love.**

How beautiful those words were to me. They brought an honesty and heartfelt truth with them. My prayer time with you is totally free of a sense of duty. It is also time-free. I don't have a set time or a set place for prayer. I can touch base with you at any time and there you are. The surrendering to love has happened. The belonging is from before time. It is eternal.

You have been doing a lot of thinking, haven't you? Your understanding of a love relationship with me is refreshing for both of us. I'm glad you don't relate to me out of duty. I never relate to you or to anyone out of duty, only out of love. To surrender to true love is to know total freedom.

Lord, one of the things I've never felt right about was where the Bible says to fear the God-part of your godliness. I can marvel and stand in awe of the God-part. I can respect, worship and adore the magnificence of God. I am aware of my minuteness in comparison. Somehow, I can melt into God's presence – but to be scared or fearful just doesn't marry with what you taught about God. When I looked at Psalms the other day I was delighted. I found fear translated as trust and obey. That really made sense to me. The call to trust and obey spoke to me of a love relationship and not a fear relationship. You really exemplified trusting and obeying God in your life. Nowhere in the Bible have I discerned that you feared God in your earthly life. That is of great comfort to me.

God really does want to be at-one with His creation. To surrender to His love out of free choice is the greatest gift or opportunity that has been given to the whole of creation. There are no boundaries, or limits, or duties. Breathe in God's love. It is eternal.

The dance of the known and the unknown ...

Lord, I come before you in worship and awe that is totally immersed in love. We have so few words to explain the different types of love we experience. The love I am trying to put into words has a sense of completeness that comes from the core of my being and encompasses the whole of creation. You are at the centre, and you are a dance of the community of you. Somehow, you are all pervading and yet all elusive, unable to be grasped and yet a part of me. Once again I come across the indefinable: the dance between the known and the unknown. I have such a peace in the mysterious, unexplainable presence of you that carries the weightlessness of me. How great is the mystery of you. How deep is the depth of you.

You are discovering the mystery of me. I am in both the known and the unknown. Keep practising my presence for I am with you always. Your at-one-ment is assured.

An eternal love ...

After I wrote our last conversation, it struck me that I had come to the end of this collection of writings. Somehow, it emerged that you had taught me what you wanted me to know at this point in time.

And what do you think that is?

I feel as though you wanted me to uncover for myself what your message about atonement was.

So what do you think our conversations did for you?

I think you wanted me to understand that you, God, love us so much that you sent the Christ of yourself—Jesus in human form—to show us how great your love is. It is a wholly all-giving love. You showed us you were prepared to totally give the depth and the enormity of your love. You emptied yourself completely so we could see the limitlessness of your love. You gave your all freely. At-one-ment is a love beyond all measure. There is nothing more you could have given than what you gave. Amazing! You, our God, wanted us to see how much you love us. At-one-ment with you is to experience such a perfect love.

I think you did all this so we could change our initial understandings of the God we thought we knew. As humankind progressed, we developed an image of a legalistic, fearsome, easily angered, punishing God who desired blood and sacrifice in order to be appeased.

Do I think these are the characteristics of the God who wanted to walk in the garden and chat with Adam and Eve? I think not!
Do I think these are the characteristics of the God who still wants to walk in the garden and chat with us? I think not again!

Through Jesus, you cleared the way to bring the following message to us!

God's desire is for everyone to openly chat with and listen to the dance of the Trinity, just as you and I have been doing over these past months.

Sometimes people worry about the silent times when chatting with you. We all know silence doesn't stop us enjoying the company of someone we love. Silence with you can be a companionable silence. It can also be a message to wait – to wait until your peace about a situation is revealed to us. Yes, a wonderful relationship is available where we can pour out our hearts to you whilst remaining whole and loved. It is a relationship also, in which we are called to trust and obey. The obedience comes out of the inner knowledge which is freely given and to which we can freely respond. Yes, you even give us free choice as to whether we follow the wisdom or not. However, we also know we are responsible for the outcomes of not following your guidance.
Jesus, you came that we might know God's love. Your Holy Spirit is the gift that crosses the invisible barriers of our earthly existence.

I now believe God didn't need Jesus to die on the cross as a scapegoat for our sins. We needed Jesus to die to show us how much God loves us and wants to be at-one with us. God never needed to change his heart and his mind about us. We needed to change our minds and our hearts about him.

The only way we can express our thanks is to love God with all our hearts and minds and strength, and to love each other in the same way. This message of love and peace is the only way forward for humankind. Jesus told us that. Humankind has heard the message but is yet to experience living it.

> God, thank you so much for sharing this journey of chatting and reflecting. There have been times when I chatted directly to the God of your godliness. Other times I chatted to the Jesus Christ of your godliness. Then there were times I found myself chatting with your Holy Spirit. Sometimes I didn't know which being of your Trinity I was relating to. Now, I know it doesn't matter which part of the dance of you I am communicating with. You know, and that's all that matters.
>
> I realise it doesn't end here. You now want me to chat with others and share the journey so they also may discover you in the same way. Yet again, you have called me to trust and obey.
> May my journey as it unfolds be a blessing to many who want to know you.
>
> **I am with you. Trust and obey.**

*Still and deep
from me to you...*

Still and deep from me to you
my Word has come, a comfort true.
As in the depths of life one sees
a peace and strength ... just as the trees
draw water fresh from unseen flow
my voice is there for you to know
that you can rest upon my rock.

Reflect on life and take still-stock
for in the silence blessed by me
you find yourself ... refreshed and free.

We, in ways, are like the birds
who soar upon the hidden surge
of currents hidden from our eyes.

This news to us is no surprise
as when in life the depths we see
our instinct is to call to Thee.
Our weakness then is like a river ...
our choice is drift or else consider
whence we came or where we're going
discovering you within our knowing.

The symbol of the pen carries with it the hope
that the reader will have their own conversations
with God. Why? Because God is just waiting
to speak intimately to each person in a way that
brings love and acceptance into their lives.

I asked...

God, many people find it hard to find you. Does it have to be so difficult to find you?

He answered...

**Just think of me and there I am.
I am within your mind and your heart,
listening and waiting for you to tune into
my still, quiet voice.**

Try it. Dare to ask God a question.
Then listen to the first thoughts that come into
your mind and write them down.
God is longing to have a conversation with you.

RUTH HAMMOND

SOFT WHISPERS... SMALL SHOUTS... DEEP WATERS...

Soft Whispers is a collection of 66 inspirational writings that are an encouragement for life's journey and an encouragement of God's love for you and the people around you. These writings, which have led to the production of the book have been a 28yr+ journey of listening and obedience. I hope for the book to be an inspiration, an encouragement, and most of all a "soft whispers, small shouts, deep waters" experience of our loving God to all. —**Ruth Hammond**

The origins of this unusual book began when Ruth was woken from sleep one night by a soft voice calling her to get up and write. She recounts: 'Words flew into my mind. Pictures filled my imagination. Insights into the depths of emotional hurts that people were carrying entered the core of my being.' It deserves to be placed on a coffee table or beside one's bedside for regular referral, and to be shared with those going through the storms of life. —**Julia Martin, Christian Writer Magazine**

RUTH HAMMOND believes writing is something that captured her some years ago. Words came into her mind and she knew she had to get them recorded. Following the death of her husband and twenty five years later the death of a son she experienced the power of the comfort contained in the words she had been given. Writing is not something she has consciously chosen to do. It seems to her that it is something she has been given to record. She felt nudged by God to produce this book, so she recorded her conversations with God to see what would eventuate. Yet again she felt amazed at the insights she received. She confesses to a feeling of bemusement at the whole process but also feels led to trust and obey the nudges she has received. Her first book 'Soft whispers... small shouts... deep waters...' has ministered to many.

This book also will speak to the hearts of its readers.

Please direct any queries to Ruth Hammond:
hello@softwhispersbook.com

www.ingramcontent.com/pod-product-compliance
Lightning Source LLC
Chambersburg PA
CBHW062028290426
44108CB00025B/2819